Dating YOUR MATE

RICK BUNDSCHUH
DAVE GILBERT

ILLUSTRATIONS BY RICK BUNDSCHUH

HARVEST HOUSE PUBLISHERS
Eugene, Oregon 97402

DATING YOUR MATE

Copyright © 1987 by Harvest House Publishers
Eugene, Oregon 97402

Library of Congress Catalog Card Number 87-080286
ISBN 0-89081-598-4

Printed in the United States of America.

Contents

♥

Dating
YOUR MATE

Introduction

♥

This book is all about romance. Its whole purpose is to ignite the fanciful, sentimental, glamorous, wild, and emotional areas of your relationship with your lover. It is our observation that many relationships endure a few years, and then the flame that once burned with such intensity dies down to a couple glowing embers. This book is intended to get your creative juices flowing and to blow new enthusiasm over those embers.

We believe romance can be as much a part of a 50-year marriage as it can be part of a honeymoon. It all depends on the amount of energy and effort that each person is willing to put into keeping the flame alive.

The ideas contained in this book will offer some fuel for love's fire. The ideas are not magic remedies guaranteed to repair a relationship falling apart, nor are they secret potions that will always succeed in winning the heart of some potential partner. But if there is a spark, many of the resources that follow can be a great help. Inside this book, you will find a variety of dating ideas (each one tried and proven effective by the authors), that will help you say "I love you" in a creative and memorable fashion.

A few tips before you explore the contents of this book.

- ♥ *Don't overdo it.* It is not necessary to employ a wild and crazy date every weekend or to always be doing the unusual. Add enough to spice up life. Save things to use later.
- ♥ *Plan ahead.* Because many of the ideas take preparation and time, it is important to do a good job setting up the date.
- ♥ *Hide this book.* Make your mate think that you are the most creative person who walks the face of this earth.

If he asks you where you got the ideas for the date just say, "Oh, I read it somewhere."

TAKE NOTE OF DIFFERENCES

Before embarking on any kind of creative activity with your mate keep in mind the differences between men and women, especially in their thinking and perceptions.

Even though men and women are alike in many areas and have the same intellectual and sometimes physical capacities, there seems to be a difference in the "wiring" of the two sexes. Therefore, we must be sensitive to the difference in thinking and perspective that each person has when dating. What may seem fun and exciting to one spouse may be totally boring to the other.

In the giving and receiving of messages between the sexes, and particularly with the dust of the Women's Liberation Movement beginning to settle, several generalities seem to be clear. With few exceptions these differences are worldwide, suggesting that in the final sifting a man and woman from the other side of the globe think and react with remarkable similarity.

In dating, engagement, marriage, and sex, men are still seen (or would like to be seen) *by women as the initiators.* This is not to say that a woman never initiates but that it is usually perceived as more "romantic" when the man initiates. Even in marriage most women would rather have their husband set up a romantic evening out on the town than have to do it themselves.

Therefore it is up to the man, if he wants to please his spouse, to figure out what signals will be received by her as romantic and initiate the action.

Another basic truth is that women like courtesy and chivalry (doors opened, help with putting coat on, heavy bags carried). There is no doubt that women are capable of doing all these things themselves. But this kind of social etiquette is seen by an overwhelming number of women as an indicator of caring.

It is not just single women who desire such courtesy, but women who are married as well. Often the married ones have learned to live with reality and don't expect it anymore.

Another classic example of the difference in perception is that most women are emotions-oriented and most men are goal-oriented. This works its way into various poses in a relationship and influences things such as gift-giving, social activities or dates, friendships, and work situations. The ability to stretch into the frame of reference of the opposite sex from time to time can enhance communication with your mate and can even enable you to have a good time doing something you normally would not choose to do.

For example, a woman may find the idea of a traditional picnic wonderfully romantic, while the man may find the weather questionable, the ground hard, and the ants annoying. The same man will have no objection to the same hardships if he happens to be going duck hunting . . . but that is because there is an objective to being on the hard ground and putting up with ants and inclement weather. He sees no point to the picnic unless he can try to understand the event through the eyes of the woman.

As silly as the old fairy tales of knights and princesses may seem, these stories have a great deal to do with how the individual outlooks of men and women may be explained. A man has been raised to be a knight. His job is to rescue a damsel from treacherous dragons, for which he will be rewarded with her eternal love. The dragon and the rescue also appeals to most men, even though the damsel is always the ultimate prize.

In contrast, a woman is the damsel in the tower waiting to be rescued. The real part of her story takes off after all the fun is over for the man. She is the prize and gets to live happily ever after simply because the man who won her was willing to slay dragons for her safety and love . . . and that kind of a knight is tough to come by.

The fun comes if you try to imagine yourself in the role of a knight (if you are a woman) or the damsel (if you are a man) and see how you might think and act if you got stuck in the wrong role for a moment.

Simplistic, no doubt, but the thrill of the battle and rescue can be revived when the knight polishes up his armor and the damsel responds with the gratitude of someone who was about to be the lunch of some overgrown reptile.

The way to the heart of our lover lies in realizing that there are two sets of expectations, two ways of perceiving and synthesizing messages, and two ways of seeing reality. We must try to tune into what will create a signal of love that can be received and recognized by our mate.

Even for those who "humbug" romance and don't feel the creative or adventurous type, positive results will come from investing a bit of thought and effort into the life of the one you married. Sure, dating is work! It takes time, preparation, planning, boldness, resourcefulness, and another person to love. But it's worth it! Not only will your mate enjoy the time, but so will you. Few things are as rewarding as the appreciative smile on your mate's face after you have successfully pulled off a special date created just for your spouse. So go ahead, take your mate on that special night out. It's worth the risk!

Creative
Dating

Creative Dating

Continuing courtship is an element that makes any relationship have vibrancy and growth. Unfortunately, many fall into a pattern of behavior that almost seems to take their mate for granted. Doing things together almost seems a chore rather than a joy. Other priorities gradually replace the first love that was shared. Reestablishing a "date" life can help refocus attention back to our mate.

Some couples who enjoy activity together find themselves stuck in the same rut of dinner and a movie (sometimes they go to a movie and then to dinner). A little thought and effort can open up new doors and possibilities of great times to share together.

Use the following ideas sparingly (like seasoning). Make sure to select the one that fits your personality or situation. Some of the dates suggested may be too radical for your personality or too far-out for your spouse to really enjoy.

Create new dates that work better for you and your lover. Edit, combine, customize—but be sure to have fun!

LET'S MAKE A DEAL

On a piece of cardboard create a three-door game that will let your lover select the place and price level of subsequent outings. Label the doors 1, 2, and 3. Behind each door write the description of a particular date (for instance, "A dinner at [a favorite restaurant] followed by a night at the theater seeing a live play"). Behind another door may be a less extravagant date such as "A fun-filled evening shopping for a new pair of shoes (on me, of course)". The last alternative might be something like "You've won an exciting evening at home with two videos of your choice and a bowlful of popcorn."

You can switch the cards around after your lover chooses and replace the date selected with a new idea in the same price range.

Make this like the TV game by first giving your lover a gift of $20 to go out with or to trade back for a chance at the doors.

MUG FOR THE CAMERA

Spend the evening with your lover taking outrageous photos in a photo booth. Invest a few dollars and get one strip of pictures with the two of you doing goofy poses, one strip of the two of you wearing funny hats and glasses, etc. Or come up with a plot for a pantomime and try to tell a story using the pictures and whatever props you have on hand. Who knows—your pictures may come out so well that you will want to have your photo-booth prints framed and hung!

PORTABLE RESTAURANT

You will need the help of friends for this one. Find an unusual setting (i.e. a crowded shopping mall or the top of a building) or a romantic spot (ocean cliffs or a secluded lakeside location) and set up a table (a card table works nicely). Tell your date to dress up because you're going to a very well-known place for dinner. When you arrive, have your friends dressed appropriately as waiters and the table set with china and candles. As you eat, be sure to compliment the impeccable service and comment on the ambiance of the place. (FOOD TIP: You could have someone be the chef and barbecue your food or simply bring it in from a nearby restaurant that has prepared it "to go." Another solution is to fix some item that can be easily kept for several hours, such as cracked crab salad on ice.)

HAWAII AT 20-BELOW

In the dead of winter surprise your mate with a luau in the living room. Get some Hawaiian music, sand and water in a jar, fruit drinks (served in coconuts with straws), roasted pork, and flower leis. (Most florists will throw something together for you that at least will resemble a lei.) Be sure to turn the thermostat to 80 degrees. It's important that you dress for the occasion. Shorts and a Hawaiian shirt would be great. If you have been to the islands, dig out some old pictures or project your slides on the wall. Visit a travel agent and talk him out of a poster or two. If you can afford it, cap off the evening with tickets to you-know-where.

THE BEST ????? IN TOWN

For a fun way to figure out where to go out to eat, agree to try and find the best of a certain kind of food in town.

For instance, you may want to discover who has the best pizza in town. Every time you go out to eat, try another pizza place. For added fun create scorecards and rate the food, service, and atmosphere. You may have the waitress and maitre d' convinced you are food critics for *Bon Appetit*.

You can play this with any specific kind of food (such as pizza) or category of food (i.e. Italian).

Make sure to hit all the restaurants in town that specialize in the food you are testing. You never know—sometimes the "dives" turn out to have the best food.

SCORE CARD

RESTAURANT NAME:

FOOD CLASS:

	A	B	C	D	F
TASTE	☐	☐	☐	☐	☐
TEXTURE	☐	☐	☐	☐	☐
SERVICE	☐	☐	☐	☐	☐
PRICE	☐	☐	☐	☐	☐
ATMOSPHERE	☐	☐	☐	☐	☐

COMMENTS _____

_____

_____

_____

SAILING . . . TAKES ME AWAY

Something about a sailboat is romantic. Rent a small sailboat and cruise the harbor for a special afternoon. It is not hard to get the hang of it and it is fun to learn together. (Be prepared to get wet and don't go outside the harbor.) If you are not near a harbor or lake big enough to sail on, try a rowboat or a canoe. Don't forget to pack a good lunch (in a waterproof container) and bring along a camera.

For added fun you can give yourselves ranks and pretend that you are on an old schooner.

ETHNIC DATES

Dress in the kind of clothing worn by the people whose food you'll be eating that night (i.e. Chinese, Mexican, French, Italian, etc.) Try to talk in that language (or at least heavily accented English) all night.

GAME BOARD DINING

Create a game board with restaurants that both of you enjoy. You can also add who has to pick up the bill and who has to drive the car. Have your lover roll dice to find out where you will be dining that evening. Have the restaurants on the board run the gamut from fast-food joints to high-class eateries.

THE LOVE BOAT

Tell your lover that you are going to take him on a cruise tonight. Drive to the nearest ferry. Act as if this is what you were talking about when you said "cruise." After you are believed, show your lover the real thing: a trip for two on a cruise ship or an evening on a dinner ship.

THE LOVE BOAT REVISITED

Rent, borrow, or beg the use of a yacht or boat for the night. (You do not have to leave the berth.)

Set up the boat in advance with provisions. (Seafood is somehow an appropriate choice.) Enjoy a candlelight dinner in the galley or a barbecue on the deck. Bring along a portable tape deck with your favorite music, a comforter, and an interesting book and snuggle together in the cabin.

A PHOTOGENIC DATE

Spend the evening shooting pictures of each other individually and together with the help of a tripod and timer. (If you do not have a camera with these accessories, you can borrow or rent them.) Drive to romantic spots or set up shots at home that have an intimate feel. After you "shoot," drop the film off at a one-hour photo developer and go out for a snack. Pick up the developed film and spend the rest of the evening mounting or framing the photos you like best. (Make sure to have frames and mounting board ready.) Or decide which one you want to use for next year's Christmas picture.

For an added twist, use a Polaroid camera and ask strangers to take pictures of the two of you at various locations.

FISH OR CUT BAIT

Tell your mate that you want to go out with him to get a fresh fish dinner. Then go to the local lake, pier, or trout farm and fish for your dinner. Clean and cook the fish there. Hide a portable barbecue in the trunk of the car along with accompaniments such as potato salad, baked beans, and pickles. Don't forget the eating utensils, cookware, plates, and beverages.

Make sure to bring along a change of clothes for your mate since fishing can be a messy and smelly business. If you are going fishing at night, bring along a warm jacket or sweater for each of you.

Cheap
Dates

Cheap Dates

There has been a time for most of us when all we had left in our wallets was the lining but we still wanted to do something fun with our mate. If you find yourself in this situation (or if you are Ebenezer Scrooge out on your first date) you may find some of these ideas helpful.

LET'S GO MALLING

Turn a shopping trip to the mall into a date! Give each other an imaginary $1000 (any amount will do) and share with each other what you would buy. Or agree on spending no more than a certain amount of money and go off and try to find a surprise gift for each other. If whatever you each select doesn't fit or match any color known to man, it can be returned on the spot.

CARD LOOKING

Go into a card shop and choose special cards to give to each other . . . only don't buy them. Just pick them out and give them to each other in the store. (Don't sign them, either!)

SHELL HUNTING

Take a trip with your lover to the seashore for the sole purpose of looking for seashells. (This can be done all year 'round since you are not going to swim.) Take a lunch, goodies for a barbecue, or plan on eating at some seashore diner.

After you have collected your shells, try to think of ways to make them special collectables. For example: Glue a magnet on the back and use them for note holders on the refrigerator. Glue them to mounting board and frame them with a picture of the two of you (at the seashore, if possible). Or carefully drill a hole in some small shells and make a pair of earrings.

COOKIE MAKERS

Make creating cookies or other goodies a whole-day project for the two of you.

First browse through cookbooks and decide what you want to bake. Go to the store together and stock up on the ingredients you will need.

Put on aprons and create delicious goodies for Christmas or for any other excuse you can think of. You may want to call for a pizza to be delivered since you probably won't feel like cooking dinner after messing up the kitchen all day.

SNOWFRIEND

If you live where it snows, this can be a fun joint project. Go to a friend's house while they are gone and make a snowman that looks like them in their front yard. (If you can get your hands on any of their clothing, use it to dress up your snowfriend.)

WHAT'S HIS LINE?

On the way to a destination or for something to do on a dull evening, make a game out of guessing what the other people you pass do for a living or where they are going. You can extend this to guessing what their name might be ("That one looks like an 'Irving,' dear") or what kind of pet they may have.

REGRESS TOGETHER

Buy some crayons and a coloring book. Take your time and color a page or two. Make sure to stay in the lines and to sign your work. This activity is perfect for by the fire on rainy, cold, or snowy nights. Self-portraits can be fun to do. Or get some old magazines and erase the eyes and teeth of the people on the cover and then "retouch" them with a pencil or felt pen. Or put a puzzle together (the tougher, the better). Add some hot chocolate, exotic coffee blends, or different kinds of tea and homemade cookies.

TUNNEL OF LOVE

Sit in the car with your lover while going through a car wash. Build up the event by telling your mate you know where there is a romantic tunnel of love. Enjoy the waterfall, a few private moments together, and get the car clean at the same time.

RAINY-DAY GOLF

When it rains it's a perfect time to go miniature golfing. If the place closes you may be able to play free. (Ask the manager if it's okay and bring your own balls and clubs.) Dress warm and and don't forget your umbrella. This is a cheap date that doubles as an adventure. (You can even forget the golf and just splash in the puddles.)

BIKERS

Plan a day of just cruising your bikes around a particular neighborhood or interesting area. (If you do not have a bike or are away from home, rent or borrow bikes.) Stop often for pictures. If riding in a residential area, choose your favorite landscaping or house architecture. When you stop for lunch, put together all of your ideas and build your dream house together.

TRIP TO THE ZOO

Try this one especially after your lover has had a frustrating time at work. Go to the zoo. Spend the afternoon renaming the animals after people with whom he or she works.

VIDEO MOVIES

For those who would like to see a certain movie but are really low on funds, try going to the video store and asking them to allow you to preview that movie right there in the store. As long as the store is open (most are till 9:00 P.M.), they'll let you stay and watch. Bring your own popcorn.

THE DRIVE-IN

Take your lover to see a drive-in movie—only this one is really different. Drive back to your house, pull out a Super-8 projector from the trunk, and show some of the old home movies of you as a kid (playing in the tub, going to the zoo, birthday parties, etc.).

Show them right there on the garage door (put the projector on the roof of the car). Plan on an intermission where you can go into the house and get popcorn and Cokes (prepared in advance, of course). If you don't have any movies, slides will also work.

GAMES FOR TWO

There are a number of games that are just perfect for two people to play. This kind of activity is great for an "indoor" day or a lazy afternoon. Learn together how to play a new game or teach each other how to play a game the other does not know. Add to the fun by making a prize or a penalty for the winner and loser. For example: If he wins, she must wash his car. If she wins, he must take her out to dinner the next night. No cheating is allowed (unless you are really getting beat badly). No poor sportsmanship should be permitted (such as hurling the chess pieces at the victorious opponent).

The following is a partial list of games that can be played by two people:

Aggravation	Cribbage
Backgammon	Parcheesi
Boggle	Pente
Checkers	Rummy Tile
Chess	Scrabble
Chinese Checkers	

Various card games
Various video games (Pac Man, Centipede, etc.)

HEAD DIP

Treat your lover to a long, gentle shampoo, scalp massage, and conditioning. Make sure to set up the bathroom like a hair salon complete with towels, chair, shampoos, conditioners, combs, and brushes.

Bring in a portable tape deck and play gentle music while you work on your favorite client.

OLD-TIME CINEMA

Find some vintage or classic movies to watch on TV or rent a video and make an evening of watching some old films. Make popcorn and snuggle under a comforter. For a variation on this idea you could pick a famous director (such as Alfred Hitchcock) and try to watch one of his films each week until you have seen them all.

A WALK ON THE BEACH

A simple and inexpensive activity is taking a walk on the beach at sunset or even at night. Roll up your pant legs and plan to get a little wet and sandy. Finish the evening with a mug of some warm beverage.

BUILD A POND

On a warm summer day go into the back country, find a stream, and build a pond together to wade or swim in by damming up the stream at a critical point. Be sure to bring some food and beverages since playing beaver is tough work. Before you leave remember to dismantle the dam.

BOAT RACES

On a day with heavy rains build a little boat for each of you out of milk cartons and race them in the gutter outside your house. Make a challenge out of it with the loser having to reward the winner with a back massage or by going to the winner's choice of movie.

NIGHT SWIM

On a warm evening go swimming at night. If swimming in the ocean, use caution to check sea conditions before venturing out. (Night ocean swimming is very weird because you cannot see the swells until they wash over you.) Find a deserted portion of a lake or arrange to use the pool of a friend when he is not home.

JUST FOR YOU

Together make a trip to the local library to try and find a poem that expresses your feelings for your lover. Write it down and present it to each other later that evening.

The
Picnic

The Picnic

The good old-fashioned traditional picnic hasn't gone out of style, just out of practice. Make it a surprise with all of the goodies packed away in the trunk of the car (blanket, beverages, fried chicken, salad, watermelon, homemade ice cream, chocolate chip cookies, etc.). A real picnic basket with full place settings for two has real class (not to mention romance).

This can be done as a surprise lunchbreak (arrange with the boss to keep your lover out of the office for an extra half hour) or as the main event of a weekend.

The success of the picnic will be assured if you have a special area already picked out.

If you plan a picnic as a surprise, don't forget to throw in an extra sweater for your lover in case it gets cool.

THE BIG CHILL

Plan a picnic during the dead of winter out on a frozen lake or pond (make sure it is frozen solid) or in the midst of a snow-covered park.

Take folding chairs, an ice chest full of warm sandwiches (obviously no ice), and munchies. Include a thermos of hot cider, coffee, or chocolate.

Depending on the weather, this may be a short picnic followed by a warm-up next to the fire or a fun-filled day of ice fishing or ice-skating.

HIDDEN PICNIC

Hide your picnic goodies in advance along a trail or in a secluded spot (or have an accomplice place your basket). Walk or ride horseback to the picnic spot and surprise your lover with a full-blown picnic. (Food in plastic containers is suggested, plus a polite note to anyone who happens to stumble upon the goods before you arrive.)

SAILBOAT PICNIC

Rent or borrow a small sailboat, motorboat, or rowboat. Take the boat offshore and enjoy a picnic. Make it an evening picnic and enjoy the sunset together.

WHAT TO PACK FOR A PICNIC

Naturally a picnic is not a real picnic without some sort of picnic basket (this can be as romantic as the old-fashioned wicker basket or as modern as the plastic ice chest). But what do you put in it?

The best rule of thumb is to put in things that you are sure both of you will enjoy. It is best to have all food prepared beforehand. Some of the things you may wish to include are:

Fried chicken
Submarine sandwiches (or sandwiches of any variety, loaded with goodies)
Fruit such as apples, oranges, tangerines, or slices of water-melon
Cheese and crackers
Chips and dip
Dessert (cookies travel better than chocolate cake or pies)
Chilled beverages and PLENTY OF ICE
Don't forget eating utensils, a blanket, and napkins.

Cooking over an open campfire is always fun. Make sure to bring firewood, starter fuel, and matches. You can roast hot dogs, cook hamburgers, or fry fresh fish (that you just caught in the river or lake). Don't forget roasted marshmallows or s'mores for dessert.

Dates for Two or More

Dates for
Two or More

❤

Often an enjoyable evening involves doing something with another couple. While not usually as romantic, these dates can be great fun (especially if you know the couple well and are willing to risk doing some crazy things together). Some of these dates are great to go on with a couple who is new to you. You will find out quickly what kind of people they really are on some of these creative dates for doubles.

SENIOR DOUBLE DATE

Double date with an older couple (i.e. 70-plus years old). Find out what they think would be a fun date. Make it a point to listen to the wisdom that comes with folks this age and to take any tips you can if they have celebrated a golden anniversary or two.

NIGHT CROQUET

Play croquet at night with flashlights. This is a good one to include several other couples on. Make it especially festive by taping different colors of cellophane over the flashlight lenses for the Malibu-light effect.

TUBING

Find a slow-moving river and borrow some inner tubes. Arrange to have one car left at the exit place on the river while you drive together to the launch spot. Bring a floating cooler and enjoy a relaxing day on the river with your friends. Don't forget life jackets and be sure you are familiar with that stretch of river.

THE GROUP DRIVE-IN

Get a bunch of friends, a pickup truck, several blankets, and stock up on your favorite popcorn, beverages, and a thermos of coffee. Go to the drive-in, back the truck into the space, and "kick back" together. You may find that you spend more time talking and acting like a bunch of sophomores than you do watching the movie.

DESSERT PARTY

The more the merrier at this one. Admission to the party is some outrageous dessert. Each couple contributes a dessert that feeds at least six. Have each person sample all the entries (except his own) and vote for the best one. An appropriate prize can be given to the winner. End the evening with a whipped cream pie-eating contest.

THE HEARTY PARTY

Have each couple bring a large volume of a single food item to combine for a huge feast (i.e. five pounds of coffee, ten pounds of beans, five gallons of chocolate ice cream). Everyone should get involved with the preparation. It is important that each guest comes or he (and his food item) will really be missed.

BOWLING IN STYLE

After a formal date, go bowling! Most bowling alleys have special late-night rates and bowling shoes look great with formal dresses or a tux. This date works best if neither of you bowl very often. This way it's just weird enough to be fun. It also guarantees that you will be the center of attention. This is also a good idea for a double date with some other wild-and-crazy-type people.

NOAH'S ARK PARTY

Invite other couples to this one and have them come in costume as twos of some animal. Each couple should bring a "natural" snack and drink only water. (If you want to be classy, drink imported sparkling water.) Make the punch bowl look like a watering trough. Be imaginative on this one. After the party you may want to go out on the town together and really freak people out.

Quick
Dates

Quick Dates

Often there isn't time for a full-blown date but there is a need to do something together alone. The following ideas can generally be done in an hour or less. Many times a neighbor can be induced to watch the kids for that length of time or the date can be squeezed in before one party goes off to work the swing shift.

THE 30-MINUTE HOT TUB

Take 30 minutes to sit in a hot tub together (if you do not have one, ask to borrow a friend's). Make sure to arrange to have the tub heated in advance. If you are going to drive to a friend's home, put your bathing suits on under your clothes to save time, and remember to bring a change of clothes. (It is a good idea to clue your friend in on the idea that this is a private date between you and your spouse so he doesn't feel the need to provide you with his company.)

Relax together and talk for the 30 minutes. Try to finish the day without falling asleep.

VIDEO WAR

Take your lover to a video arcade and the two of you learn to play a game you have never played before. See who can beat who in total points (don't play anything else). The winner has to treat for ice cream on the way home.

DUCK FEED

Take your spouse out to feed the ducks at a local pond or lake. Make sure to bring a bag of bread crumbs with you and maybe a snack for you to eat as well.

TOGETHER WORKOUT

Set a routine up where you jog, walk, do sit-ups, or lift weights together. Not only will you share an activity but you will probably lose some pounds, too.

THE FORMAL GOLDEN ARCHES

Dress up formally and go out to McDonald's. You will have little other choice if you want to keep the date within the time frame of an hour.

BUBBLE BLOWERS

Get a couple of bottles of bubble stuff and the two of you go up on the roof and blow bubbles. (Pull the ladder up after you so that you can be insured of your privacy.) Or if you need to get away from home, drive to a park or go to the top of a tall building and blow bubbles there.

RIDE ELEVATORS

Go to a nearby high-rise building and ride the elevators (getting off on the top floor to enjoy the view is optional). You can have a race with each other to see who gets to the top first. The loser has to buy the winner a treat on the way home.

SWINGERS

Take your mate on a quick date by going to the park and swinging together on the playground equipment. See who can get the highest without flying out of the swing.

15 MINUTES NORTH

Take a drive, bike ride, or jog as far north as you can get in 15 minutes, then turn around and come back. You can do this in all directions and even create a map showing how far you got on each adventure.

Big-Time
Date$

Big Time
Date$

Once in awhile it is fun to pull out all the stops and pretend that you have an unlimited amount of cash to spend on your lover. These are the big once-in-a-lifetime extravaganzas that leave a big impression. Of course, for some people money is no object. For both the one-timers and the Daddy Warbucks, the following ideas will make your lover feel like a million.

GO IN STYLE

Sometimes the location of a date is not as exciting as the means to get there. Many people have rented limousines for an evening, but you may want to think about some other unique transportation as well. For example, a horse-drawn carriage is interesting and romantic. Maybe you could ride horses to your destination. A motorcycle with a sidecar would be exciting. An antique car might be preferred by others. These and many other vehicles are available for rent and often for much less than you would expect.

GO SOME PLACE OUTRAGEOUS

For a wild vacation or prolonged "date" take your spouse on one of these adventures:

Ski Mauna Kea in the morning and lay on the beach in the afternoon.

Join a photo safari to Africa or India.

Try an underwater photo safari in the Bahamas or South Seas.

Visit all the countries in a certain section of the world (for instance, Europe). Have a picture of yourself-taken in front of each of their government headquarters.

Take the train across the USA or Europe, or catch the Orient Express.

Go to a play on Broadway.

Visit Transylvania.

For a lot more expensive trips, see your travel agent and tell him you want a vacation to remember.

HELIODATE

Rent the services of a helicopter pilot to cruise you around your city. A fun way to approach this date is to coax your mate into going with you to "check out the city." If you have the time and money you can get the pilot to drop you off at an inaccessible spot for a picnic lunch and then pick you up later.

INTERSTATE LUNCH

Take advantage of airfare specials by planning to have dinner or lunch in another city or state. Check with your travel agent to see if this exotic date will fit into your budget. When you arrive, rent a car and take a quick tour of the city before you eat.

This can also be a great mystery date. Most lovers would never expect to be taken away on a plane for dinner.

FULL OF HOT AIR

Take your lover on a date that will be remembered for a long time—a flight on a hot-air balloon. Check in your area for the availability of balloon flights.

Surprises

Surprises

To ambush your mate with love is the object of surprises. Therefore these dates depend on secrecy—and if you have a Sherlock Holmes for a mate, cleverness—for the effect to work its best magic.

Timing is also a consideration when pulling off a surprise. To plan a special event when your lover has unchangeable plans or is drowning in other commitments may cause more tension than enjoyment.

As with other ideas in this book, surprises may have more impact and returns for your lover if they are done publicly. For more fun, send flowers to your mate's workplace. It's always a special treat for everyone else at work, too, trying to guess who the flowers are from and what the occasion is. Some of the surprises listed are ones that can be done in many variations over and over again; others are surprises that you may spring only once or twice in a lifetime. But one thing for sure, being surprised by love is the best surprise of all.

RANSOMED TEDDY

Lift an item of sentimental value from your lover such as an old teddy bear or favorite picture.

Send a ransom note cut out of letters from magazines stating that the existence of the beloved bear is threatened unless you are met at a particular time and place (such as a restaurant). Be waiting there and return the teddy bear with a bouquet of flowers in his little paws.

NAME THAT TUNESMITH

Set up this surprise by playing the song of one of your lover's favorite recording artists in the background and casually striking up a conversation about your mate's work. Ask an off-the-cuff question such as "Do you think [the artist's name] is as good live as on a recording?" After your mate responds, pop out tickets to the recording artist's concert and announce "Well, I guess we will have to see for ourselves!"

A CHANGE IN MENU

Before taking your lover to some special restaurant, get a copy of the menu. Take it to a local typesetter and have the entrée or salad changed and put your own special message there. Instead of a salad description, the menu might read "Jill, I love you and I'm glad you decided to spend your life with me, HAPPY ANNIVERSARY, Jim." Arrange the switch ahead of time with the waiter who will be serving your table.

BREAKFAST IN BED

A lot of people talk about doing this but few get around to it. Do it right: Pick up a nice bed tray, a flower in a vase, the morning newspaper, and all the meal fixin's.

WEEKEND WHIRLWIND

Take your spouse away for the weekend without his prior knowledge. Secretly farm out the kids, pack both of your bags, and hide them in the car. Make reservations at a nice hotel and have flowers waiting. Don't say where you are going . . . make your mate guess. This one is worth every penny.

WHY? BECAUSE WE LOVE YOU

If your lover has been through a tough time or needs some encouragement, secretly call a bunch of his friends and arrange an appreciation party. Select a large card and have everyone write something meaningful in it. Put banners up and have a cake decorated with loving thoughts. After the party take your mate to a quiet place and tell him how much he means to you.

BREAKFAST KIDNAP

Kidnap your spouse for breakfast. Surprise is the key to this one. Get up early and steal him right out of bed (pj's and all, if you can) and take him to a restaurant. (As with all other surprises, make sure you arrange a baby-sitter or drop the kids off at a prearranged house on the way.) Do this on a weekday when your mate least expects it. (You may have to arrange with his boss to allow him to be a little late that morning.)

If kidnapping is completely out of the question, arrange for breakfast to be catered to you at home. This can be done by a professional caterer or by a friend who is in cahoots with your plan.

TERRORIST KIDNAP

Have some friends dress up in black suits (with stockings or ski masks pulled over their heads), surprise your loved one and kidnap, blindfold, and deliver him to a surprise dinner date or party in his honor. (Make sure that this is *clearly* done in fun.) Use water pistols and let your target know that this is a gag that he is expected to go along with or face a deadly stream of water. Don't try this with someone who sleeps with guns or who has Mafia connections. (It may be wise to warn the neighbors so that no vigilante action is taken.)

30 DAYS OF SURPRISES

Select a month to bring (or send, if you can afford the postage) a surprise a day. Be as clever as possible in selecting the gift. Make your selections thoughtfully. (It helps to write out what things you want to buy and then go shopping for them.) The surprises do not have to be costly. They can be free (such as a twenty-minute back massage). They can build on one another (such as a bud vase one day and a single rose the next). They can be humorous or symbolic of something that you love about your mate and want to express.

UP ON THE ROOF

Take the elevator to the top floor of a tall building and gain access to the roof. (It's a good idea to get the permission and setup for this done in advance.) Bring a tape deck for music, a basket of food and beverages, and dance the night away under the stars. There is definitely something romantic about being on a roof on a warm evening.

VIDEO COMPLIMENTS

Get a video camera and interview your lover's friends. Have them say something about your mate's strengths and give appropriate compliments. Just for laughs interview someone your lover doesn't know but may see a lot (grocery clerk, gas-station attendant, mailperson, etc). Have the stranger go on about how wonderful your mate is. This should really stun your lover. Don't forget a special message. Play the video for your mate at a special time. This works particularly well for a birthday.

If you are skilled with splicing video tapes, wedge your interviews in as a "commercial of love" between some shows that you have taped to watch together. This is guaranteed to cause a real surprise!

SURPRISE SUBSCRIPTION

Discover the magazine(s) that your mate enjoys but does not have a subscription to. Buy the issue on the newsstand and send for a subscription. Wrap the one you bought as a gift and include a card saying that the magazine will be coming as a regular reminder of your love. (You can also subscribe without saying anything and see how long it takes your mate to figure out what is happening.)

DO-IT-YERSELF-DINNER

If you are not in the custom of preparing dinner, and especially if your lover works, take off early and make a super meal for the two of you. To pull this off you may have to be sly and look through the cookbook the day before to make sure you have the right ingredients on hand. Don't forget the cloth napkins and the candles. The cook should clean up, too.

CLEAN-CAR THIEF

While your lover is at work "steal" the car she drives, totally clean it inside and out, and return it to its parking space. For added fun buy a new tape and slip it into the tape deck and place a bouquet of flowers or some homemade goodies and a card from the "clean thief" on the front seat. Naturally this works best if you are sly enough not to get caught.

DO WHAT'S NOT YOU

Invite yourself along with your lover to some event or activity that you would normally avoid like the plague. For example, you may elect to accompany your lover as she goes to a meeting of the Orchid Society or tag along with your man as he goes fishing. (Make sure to take your Dramamine.) The whole time you are with your mate, try to give your complete attention to what he is enjoying—and even try to enjoy it yourself (no whining or rolling of eyes allowed).

Creative
Gift Buying

Creative Gift Buying

♥

FLOWERS

Giving flowers is still one of the most romantic things that a man can do for a woman.

To many men, paying money for something that is going to fall over and die in a week doesn't make a whole lot of sense. Flowers are thought of as having no real utilitarian value, only an aesthetic one.

Whether it makes sense or not, the majority of women perceive flowers as one of the highest forms of personal gifts. It tells a woman she is special in a way that touches her emotional chords.

The following tips are primarily for men who are willing but perhaps unaccustomed to venturing into a tulip patch, sidewalk stand, or flower shop. (Regular flower buyers may discover some helpful hints, too.)

1. Roses are traditionally the flower that says "I love you". Most men go straight for the long-stem, medium red roses, figuring that they better keep with tradition. But there are a lot of other options in the rose department.

Roses come in various colors and in various lengths. The small-stemmed roses are extremely beautiful and delicate, and are usually far less expensive than the larger ones. Most florists will place these in a vase with greens or small filler flowers for free or at a nominal charge. Ask for miniature roses.

If you want to get creative and still stick with roses, ask for white, pink, yellow, or talisman (an orange color). Include something in the card you send that tells why you selected the color (i.e. "Yellow reminds me of the warmth of your personality").

2. Cut flowers from local stands are often cheaper than those from florists, but the flowers usually vary seasonally.

3. One flower is better than no flowers at all. Buy a little bud vase which is designed for single flowers.

4. Send arrangements to your wife's place of work. This gives your wife the opportunity to show off what a great deal she got in you.

5. If you find yourself absolutely choking on the idea of spending money for live flowers, you may want to consider buying a silk or dried-flower arrangement. They cost a little more, but will always be around to dust. (Please note that most women would still *prefer* fresh-cut flowers.)

6. Living plants are another way to give a gift that lasts beyond the moment. Try to select a plant that has flowers in bloom.

7. If you are on a real budget, flowers can usually be had by asking the neighbor very nicely and being quick with the hedge clippers. Some women treasure far more the fresh-picked neighborhood flowers stuck in a clean jam jar than they do the professionally done variety.

8. When ordering flowers—especially roses—keep in mind that you will probably be charged the same for boxed flowers that are delivered as you would for flowers which are cut and arranged in a vase by the florist. If you don't want your spouse to have to do any work, order them already arranged.

9. Don't neglect to put a card written with very special words with your flowers. The flowers will fade away, but your spouse can keep the card as a reminder of your love.

10. A large part of gift-giving is the manner in which the gift is presented. Walking in the door and tossing the flowers at your loved one, while better than nothing, has far less impact than thoughtfully picking the moment for a gentle presentation.

FLOWERS FOR MEN

Most men only get flowers at the hospital or at their funeral. Nevertheless, some creative women have found things in the plant world that their men actually like. You might try buying a Venus flytrap or some other bizarre-behaving type of plant. If you are in love with a gardener, buy him plants or flowers that he can plug into the ground. Even guys who put on the macho act don't usually mind getting plant gifts that are utilitarian in nature or good conversation pieces.

SCENTS

Perfumes and scents have been around for thousands of years. In some cases they were the exclusive property of the rich and even a sign of wealth.

In ancient days perfume was often used to mask the wearer's body odor from lack of bathing. Occasionally it was mixed with an oil substance for combing through the hair to insure against lice and other unwelcome visitors. In other cultures, like our own, it is used to accent an already-clean body.

Almost all of us agree that the pleasant aroma of a good cologne or perfume adds to the sensual dimension of the person wearing it. Therefore it makes a perfect gift—if it happens to be an aroma enjoyed by the recipient.

If you like the scent that your lover uses and want to put it in your memory banks for a later gift-giving occasion, you can usually discover what it is by simply asking. (Most perfumes have unusual names so make sure to write it down somewhere.) The other way is to go through your mate's perfume bottles and try to figure out which one carries the scent that you like. Once again, write down the name of the perfume and the maker. (Note: Usually the one she likes best is sitting out in front of the others because of continual use.)

The way NOT to buy a scent for your lover is to cruise the perfume counter at the department store. Not only will the wild variance of scents begin to confuse your olfactory system, but if you start to dab a little on your hand to get the effect the smell has coming off skin, you'll go home smelling like you were fraternizing with the whole secretarial pool (or at the least you will muff your chance at a good solid surprise).

Occasionally someone you meet will be using a cologne that you like the smell of and would like to buy for your lover. Most people are flattered when asked what they are using that makes them smell so good and will be happy to tell you.

Keep in mind that most good colognes and perfumes are supposed to mix with the natural odors that each individual has. Therefore their makers claim that the scent will change from wearer to wearer. Also keep in mind that good cologne or perfume is expensive.

Most men are not opposed to wearing some sort of cologne or after-shave. Many simply stop doing it after a while in their relationships.

When giving scents to a man, it can be very helpful to remind him of how crazy the aroma makes you. You will probably have little trouble after that with your man getting lazy about using cologne.

THE FILE CARD

While not a surprise in itself, a file card on your lover will certainly help you know how to buy personal items for a surprise.

On a card that will fit into your wallet or purse, list all the important data about your lover. Include:

> Shirt or blouse size
> Dress or jacket size
> Shoe size
> Lingerie size
> Neck and waistline size
> Color preferences
> Favorite stones or metals
> Favorite perfumes or colognes
> Names of favorite places to shop
> Any other data such as brand of golf balls they use
> or designer whose clothes they favor

Of course this information should be gathered gradually and updated occasionally (especially after diets succeed or fail). Much of it can be gathered by innocent questioning or observation.

BIG GAME HUNTER

Make three cutouts of animals from cardboard. On the back of each write the name of something your lover needs or wants but hasn't got around to buying. (Use your creativity: If your spouse has been complaining about the bad condition of her purse, make a cutout of a cow and write "New Purse" on the back of the picture.) Then tell your lover that you are going to take her on a safari to bag something she has been after for a long time. Give her a toy dart gun with one dart. Set the cardboard figures around the house and tell her if she sees one and hits it she will be able to take her "kill" home. (You may want to establish a minimum distance from which she can shoot.) When an animal has been bagged, immediately take your lover out for a shopping spree to get the long-needed item.

TREASURE CHEST

Locate a small chest and put in it some gift your lover will appreciate. (For instance, if you are in the habit of dining out once a week it could be a meal ticket to a fancy restaurant that you would not normally go to.) Lock the chest and place the key in a bag with three similar keys. Once a week bring out the chest and let your lover play the game of trying to select the right key for the lock. (You can do this with a combination lock as well by giving the three numbers out of order.) Play weekly until your mate has won or until he threatens to beat you if you don't give him the prize.

Get the Message

Get the Message

Creative Cards, Invitations, and Love Notes

Regardless of how long a relationship has been going on, there is still something wonderfully romantic about messages of love being put down on paper. In fact, to receive a written invitation for a date somehow adds to the mystique and excitement of the event. In a sense, it makes your lover feel that you are still courting her . . . even if you have been married for years. On top of that, written expressions of sentiment are often the most valued keepsakes of the beloved. They are tangible tokens of love and can bring back a whole flood of memories when reread years later.

Written expressions take thought. And they take time and effort—but it is usually time and effort well spent. For many people, writing gives them a chance to put their feelings into precise words, something that may come with difficulty in speech. Writing also gives the loved one a chance to read and reread the message . . . and to do so whenever he needs assurance or a warm blast of emotion.

Clever invitations also take time and thought. It is certainly much easier to simply *ask* your lover if she would like to go out to dinner . . . but it is not nearly as much fun.

For couples who have been married for years, an invitation can be a source of excitement because it is so unexpected.

The ideas that follow for cards and invitations are by no means exhaustive. They may ignite some creative idea that is altogether different but 100 percent effective for your lover. All the better!

The following tips may be helpful when considering sending a card or invitation.

- ♥ Make sure to be conscious of the mail schedules, especially if a message is to reach your lover by a particular date. It can be a real disappointment to receive an invitation to a Valentine's Day dinner the day after Valentine's Day because the letter was delivered late.
- ♥ Sending the card or invitation to your loved one's place of work is usually desirable since it causes your mate to share with other people how wonderful it is having someone like you as a spouse.
- ♥ If you are using the ideas in this book to establish contact with someone you would like to date, make sure to allow her a way to escape gracefully if she would like to decline the date.
- ♥ Secrecy is the best way to go about sending cards or invitations. Resist the urge to tell your lover to "make sure to check the mailbox today" because you are so excited about what nice things you have sent.

THE POSTCARD PUZZLE

If you go on a trip where your mate cannot accompany you, buy a number of postcards the first day and write a message by spreading them out in a square pattern and continuing the message across each postcard. Mail one postcard each day out of sequence. Your lover will have to wait to get all the cards to put together the message you are sending.

MAKE YOUR OWN CARD

Design your own card by hand or by creating a collage of figures cut out of magazines. Or use things like stickers, rubber stamps, or bits of material to make a custom card. Give the card thoughts all your own. Have the card laminated so that it can be a keepsake.

THE LOVE CALENDAR

Create a calendar (or buy one and customize it) to tell your lover what you think of her 365 days a year. Create special days, try to write down significant milestones from your history together (for example, the first time you dated or met as well as anniversaries). Put sealed messages on some days (use a piece of paper and small labels or stickers to cover and seal the messages).

Wrap up the calendar and give it to your lover as a gift. Don't forget to transfer all of the special days to your calendar at home or work so that you will remember those days with a card, flowers, or a special date.

HIDDEN NOTES

Build anticipation for a special date by writing and hiding hint notes each day about that date in strategic places. Describe various aspects about the location of the date in your notes without giving away the surprise. Good places to hide hint notes are in the next day's underwear, under your mate's dinner plate, in bed, in a shoe, under a food item (not one that is too moist like rice or mashed potatoes), or on the bathroom mirror.

AT-WORK NOTES

Write a note of love and send it to your mate's place of employment. Don't wait for a special holiday—just do it because you love her and want her to know you think she is special. This will catch your mate by surprise not only because you normally don't send messages at work, but also because there is no special occasion. Be careful not to make it too sexy or revealing because it will probably be shown all around the office.

T.P. LOVE NOTES

Unroll a fresh roll of toilet paper a distance and write a message to your lover or an invitation to dinner on the tissue. Roll the paper back up and reinsert the tissue on the dispenser. Don't be surprised if one day you hear shrieks of laughter coming from the bathroom.

THE JIGSAW

Create a card, love note, coupon, or invitation in the form of a puzzle and present it unassembled to your lover.

This can be done by purchasing a jigsaw puzzle and spraying out the picture with white paint and writing in your own message with felt pens. (You will need to assemble the puzzle for this method.) You can also write or draw your card on heavy paper or card stock (or wood if you are skilled with a jigsaw), then cut the card into various geometric shapes with an X-acto or utility knife. Some assembled precut puzzles are available in card or specialty stores.

Place the disassembled puzzle in a box and wrap it as a gift, or put the puzzle in an envelope and send it through the mail. For extra fun send little bits of the puzzle in the mail each day.

The puzzle can be extremely complex or simple depending upon how frustrated you wish to get your partner.

WHERE YOU LEAST EXPECT IT

Think of a dozen things that you would like to say to your lover. Write each thought on an index card or slip of paper and secretly slip them into various articles of your mate's clothing, her jacket, purse, toes of her shoes, drawers, jewelry box—just about anywhere. (You can even cover a card with clear contact paper and put it on a pot roast in the freezer.)

This little act of thoughtfulness often pays off when you least expect it.

WORD-PUZZLE LOVE NOTE

Create a love note using a hidden-word puzzle. Send it in the mail or leave it on the pillow or taped to the steering wheel of the car. (Caution: When creating a hidden-word puzzle, check carefully for words that may be created that you don't want to say.)

```
X P X X O Y N Z Q A P O N Z H F G K I J Q P
F R P I D J M Z Z N Q U P C B A F H G N I B
Z M N P Q S T R U V T Z Q K N K T P A F R O
O B N Y O U Y O K N O W V H T H A T D G I M
K D E F G C B A F T O Z R S U V N Z Q B J R
A L O U T N D V D X O N R P C Q Z N M A F C
V M X Y Z R P O E I U T X H R A B C D B U K
Q F E Z S V I J K L L P R O A S T N V O Y H
U W B S A T V W J M N V O L Z K I J N U O F
A M Z H M M I E Q P O N M I Y S Y Q Z T U W
```

TAPED LOVE NOTE

Ask your lover to call you at a certain time and prepare a juicy bit of love talk on your answering machine. You may want to include something like the following for anyone else who happens to call during the time the machine is on: "And by the way, if you are a friend or stranger who has called, I think you can tell that we really love each other."

SEE YOU IN THE FUNNY PAPERS

Slip out and retrieve the Sunday comics early in the morning (or at the newsstand on Saturday night). Cut out slips of paper and glue them over the dialogue ballons of a comic that you know your lover reads. Write in your own dialogue in place of the conversation that was there. Use it as an opportunity to say wonderful things to your lover and surprise him at the same time.

THE PIDIDDLE

This is an old tradition that you can revive for your lover. A pididdle is a "one-eyed" car (one headlight working). Whenever you see a pididdle you may give your lover a kiss. You can also up the stakes a little. Three pididdles in one night means that you must also take turns giving each other a back massage (or whatever reward you agree on). (Note: Wait until you get home before collecting on the back massage since it is hard to drive and massage at the same time.)

NUTTY MAIL

The Post Office will mail all kinds of strange things. Write your message on a coconut with indelible marker and send it to your lover through the mail. Stunts like this are just begging for corny lines such as "You drive me Nutty!" or "I'm Ape over you." (You can think of lots more.) Your imagination and the cooperation of the Post Office are the only barriers.

A CARD A DAY

For 30 days send your mate a card a day. Cards can be great ways to tell your lover how special he is to you. You may wish to spend a great deal of time in a card store selecting the greetings you want to send. Mail the cards to your lover's workplace and make him the talk of the office. You can also create your own card or take one huge card and cut it up into 30 pieces. On the back of the envelope you can write a countdown. On Day 30, go out and do something special.

THE MULTIPLE CHOICE

Create a multiple-choice invitation to help your lover have fun choosing a date or evening out. Clever multiple-choice questionnaires can be made easily by hand, typewriter, or computer. A sample multiple-choice invitation may read as follows:

THIS INVITATION IS ISSUED TO _____ TO JOIN ME IN A FINE MEAL AT:
(Circle one)

The Velvet Turtle   Barney's Pizza Joint
The Golden Arches   Sam's Sushi
Caesar's Salads

TO BE FOLLOWED BY A GREAT TIME AT:
(Check your favorite)

____ Joe's Video Arcade
____ The Reissue of "Bambi"
____ An Evening at Off-Broadway

WOUND UP BY:
(Pick one)

____ A barefoot walk on the beach
____ Hot chocolate by the fire
____ Quiet conversation over a piece of pie

RENT A MESSAGE

Rent a message to your lover on a banner that trails behind a small plane. (Many communities have this aerial form of advertising at beaches or parks.) Make sure to get your lover to the location the plane will be flying over that day. Don't point out the message—just wait for your mate to respond . . . and he will!

ON THE WALL

Write a short love note to your mate on the wall of the shower with shaving cream. (This works best if you know she is going to take a shower soon.) Or write your note on the mirror in lipstick. Make sure to offer to clean the mirror, too.

Communication Creators

Communication Creators

♥

KNOW IT ALL

Take it upon yourself to learn as much as possible about some activity or subject in which your lover is interested (for example, needlepoint). Get books from the library and read them on the side. Talk to people who can explain the activity in layman's language. (This is especially helpful if your lover's interest is nuclear physics.) Pick a time and just start talking about the subject with your lover. He will be amazed at what you know, and thrilled that you made the effort for him.

OLDIES BUT GOODIES

Dredge out all of the old albums and tapes from the back of the stack or bottom of the pile and take an audible stroll down Memory Lane. Cook up some exotic coffee or hot chocolate and sample all the music that you used to enjoy. (It is fun looking at the album covers, too, because it is hard to believe that people actually used to dress like that.)

PENALTY CHESS

On the bottom of chess or checker pieces, tape small notes that must be read if your lover loses that piece. The notes should be some sort of love penalty. The "punishment" could be something enjoyed by both people such as "a long, passionate kiss" or something like "You take out the garbage tonight."

Anytime in the course of the game that a playing piece is lost to an opponent, the losing player must do what is written on the bottom of the piece lost or captured. With a little imagination the game can turn into a whole lot of extra fun.

CONVERSATION CARDS

Create a communication game by writing down questions that you want to hear your lover talk about on three-by-five cards. You can color-code them: white = light subject, blue = general interest, pink = philosophical, etc. Or make the cards a truth or dare (for example, "Tell your secret dream spot of the world or what kind of car you think fits your image").

Let your mate select the card(s) and put a condition that he must speak for three minutes about the subject.

Be prepared to answer the question yourself.

BACK TO YESTERDAY

Go back with your lover to when life seemed "simple." Start out the night by playing a tape of music that was popular when you were both high schoolers. As you drive to dinner, recall for each other what this song reminds you of. Eat at some place where you would have eaten when you were 17 (drive-in, hamburger stand, pizza place, etc). Do something later that night you would have done when you were in high school (t.p. a friend's house, make a fire on the beach, etc.). Make sure to dress for the occasion.

READ TO ME

Find a book that both of you would enjoy and read a chapter each evening to your spouse. Make sure to set the atmosphere: Soften the lights, put on light strains of classical music, and prepare warm beverages to sip while reading.

SLEEPYTIME

Set a weeklong tradition of turning off the TV a half hour before bedtime and talking over hot chocolate or caffeine-free tea. Who knows—it may become a permanent tradition.

RENEW YOUR VOWS

Every year you can renew your marriage commitment by reciting your original vows. If you have a videotape of your wedding, be sure to look at it. You can make things a bit more elaborate by wearing your wedding dress and tux. You might even want to invite the original minister and friends to be there to rewitness the event.

REMEMBER WHEN

On a rainy, cold, or snowy evening, light a fire in the fireplace and get out your wedding pictures and reminisce. Don't neglect the playing of love songs on the stereo. This is also a perfect time to put a scrapbook together and remember the significance of each item you choose to put inside it. (Helpful hint: Prepare in advance by buying a scrapbook, glue, and other necessities to have on hand when you want to do this activity.) Don't forget some warm brew and light munchies to round out the evening.

THE TEA PARTY

Purchase a selection of teas (the more the merrier). Prepare lots of boiling water and plenty of mugs and sit down with your lover for a tea party taste-testing to decide on your favorite tea. You may want to make a trip to the imported-food section of the grocery store and buy some English crumpets.

To add intrigue, send an invitation to your lover to join you for tea at 4:00 P.M. on a selected day. Have all the goodies waiting when he arrives.

Creative Holidays

Creative Holidays

♥

CHRISTMAS

Christmas is a wonderful time to let your lover know what he means to you. Unfortunately, because of all the hectic things to do at Christmas, time alone together often gets sacrificed. Use the holiday as an opportunity to say "I love you" creatively and to do special things together.

DECORATING DUO

Take your lover on a shopping trip specifically for Christmas decorations. Look for one special thing that will remind you for years to come of your Christmas together this year. Better yet, work together on creating homemade Christmas ornaments for your house and tree.

A DATE WITH SANTA

Surprise your lover by dressing up like Santa for your night out. It just may be that she has wanted to go on a date with Santa ever since she was a little girl. Don't forget the candy canes for the little ones who will be bugging you all night.

A CAROLING DATE

Instead of just going on a date to enjoy yourselves, get another couple or two and look for people to whom you could bring a little holiday cheer. Folks who are older, housebound, sick, or bedridden are just some suggestions. Bring a crazy instrument with you like a slide-a-phone, kazoo, or jingle bells. The results can be hilarious as well as heartwarming.

THE TWELVE DAYS OF CHRISTMAS

Using this popular Christmas carol as a model, dream up a gift a day for the 12 days prior to Christmas.

These gifts may or may not reflect the themes in the song. It can be a lot of fun using the ideas from the carol as take-off points for creative gifts.

As an example: A partridge in a pear tree doesn't make the world's most exciting gift. A dove-shaped necklace hanging in a bonsai plant might. "Two turtle doves" could be a dinner for two at the Velvet Turtle (or local fried-chicken restaurant).

Using a new Christmas card each day can help you explain your gift by saying things such as "These five golden rings are best worn in the ear" (to go with five sets of earrings) or "Ten maids a milking can make one stupendous milk shake and so will we at Zippie's Ice Cream Emporium after dinner tonight."

This kind of creative Christmas giving is only limited by your imagination and time.

THE CHRISTMAS STOCKING

A fully loaded Christmas stocking of small, thoughtful gifts can be more fun than spending big money on major-league gifts.

Sneak the stocking under the tree or by the fireplace on Christmas Eve. If you have a special gift, such as a ring, watch, or keys to a new car, make sure this goes at the bottom of the stocking toe. Then pack the stocking with small goodies that you know will be appreciated.

Here is a sample list of items that might go in a woman's stocking:

Perfume
Various sweets you know she likes
Lingerie
Fingernail polish or remover
Various hand or body creams
Bubble bath or soaps
Pocket calculators or small electronic devices such as headsets
Cassette tapes
Rolls of quarters for a shopping spree
Hair brushes or combs
Potpourri, sachets
Gloves
Pens
Paperback books
Magazines (you will need to roll these and put them in first)
Earrings, necklaces, bracelets
Belts or waist ties
Manicure set
A mug for work or home (with special slogan, college logo, etc.)
Small framed photos of you or the family
Scarfs, mittens, woolen socks
Panty hose
Small jars of exotic jams or favorite foods
AND DON'T FORGET A NOTE FROM "SANTA"

Ideas for a man's stocking:

> Cologne
> Razors
> Shaving creme or shaving brush and mug
> Combs and brushes
> Manicure set
> Scarf
> Gloves
> Socks
> Jewelry (neck chain, ring, watch, tie tack, bracelet)
> Coffee mug
> Magazines that he will enjoy
> Paperback books
> Designer briefs
> Pocket calculator or small electronic devices such
>   as headsets
> Cassette tapes
> Compact disc recordings
> Pens
> His favorite snack food or munchies
> Small tools (tape measure, drill attachments, etc.)
> Ties
> Belts
> Small framed photo of you or the family
> Wallet
> DON'T FORGET A SIZZLING NOTE FROM
>   "MRS. CLAUS"

THE CUSTOM-MADE ADVENT CALENDAR

Before Christmas, create an Advent calendar for your lover counting down the 25 days before Christmas.

Using several pieces of thin cardboard, cut one into 25 small squares (the size of business cards). Number the cards and lay them out on a large piece of uncut cardboard. Securely tape one side of the cards to create the "hinge".

Behind each card write some activity, idea, thought, or clue to the location of a gift. For example, on day one you may write a compliment to your lover such as "You have the most gentle eyes that I have ever seen." On day two, you might leave a clue to a puzzle that will (on Christmas Day) lead to some gift, such as "In the northwest corner." On day three, you could write "Don't cook tonight! We are eating out!" Other ideas could include a favorite line of verse, a Scripture, or a refrain.

Seal the door with a holiday sticker or label.

This calendar can be done quite lavishly if you have the time. For example, a calendar designed in a woodshop could be made like a shadow box but with real doors and hinges. This would allow actual small gifts to be placed in each opening.

A well-made Advent calendar can be reused every year by changing the messages behind the doors.

MISTLETOE MANIACS

If you live in a part of the country where mistletoe grows, make a special day trip out to the country to pick mistletoe for your house during the holiday season. You can make a picnic out of the trip if the weather permits or just snuggle in some out-of-the-way cafe after you have picked your mistletoe.

When you return home, make sure that you hang the mistletoe over every doorway in the house. Use it frequently.

COLUMBUS DATE

Use Columbus Day as an opportunity to have a discovery date. The theme of the day is to discover something. It can be anything from driving to a bordering town to discovering a new restaurant, to asking series of questions that will help you discover something new about each other. Another fun twist would be to get into a small boat and sail, row, or motor to a small island in the middle of a lake, discover it, name it, and have a picnic lunch there.

APRIL FOOL'S DATE

On April Fool's Day take your lover out with the understanding that sometime during the date you will play a trick on each other. Since both of you know this before you go out, the other will be expecting something to happen. This means that you will have to be all the more witty and devious.

THE DAY YOU MET

Try to remember the day you met and make it a national holiday for the two of you. Treat it just like you would an anniversary. Go out and try to duplicate your first date.

LOVE-YOU EGGS

Create love notes or clues to a hidden gift by writing the messages on eggs with a white crayon (available in any kid's room) and then dyeing the eggs various colors and hiding them around the house.

GROUNDHOG DAY

Any excuse is a good one when you are looking for things to do with your lover. Groundhog Day can offer one of these. You can go from the extravagant (flying to some place for the weekend where winter does not exist—warm or tropical climates) to the silly (go on a groundhog hunt and find a groundhog looking at himself).

For some groundhog information and paraphernalia write the Chamber of Commerce in Punxsutawney, Pennsylvania, where Groundhog Day originated. They will send you a colorful brochure that gives the history of Groundhog Day plus an order blank for all kinds of groundhog goodies such as mugs, pennants, T-shirts, and notepaper.

THE FIRST DAY OF WINTER

Make a big deal out of the first day of each season by having a celebration with your lover or by creating a party for you and other couples.

You could celebrate the first day of winter with a special card (buy the kind without a message and write your own, but make sure it has a winter feel to it) or with a gift of winter clothing such as a scarf, gloves, or sweater. Have a dessert of ice cream, snow cones, or popsicles.

For group activities you could try one of the following:

- ♥ *Snowball fight* (minus the snow)—Divide the room in half. Each couple has a stack of newspapers. To start the fight, wad the paper into a ball and throw it at those on the other side of the room until an agreed-upon time period is up. The side with the least amount of "snowballs" in their area wins.
- ♥ *Arctic blue toes*—Put marbles in a bucket of crushed ice and water. See how many each person can pull out in the allotted amount of time using only their toes.
- ♥ *Snowflakes*—See who can cut out the best-looking snow-flake from white paper. Hang these from the ceiling for atmosphere.

Don't forget that you also can create special occasions for the first day of fall, spring, and summer.

CREATE YOUR OWN HOLIDAY

Try creating your own holiday especially designed for you and your lover. Make up a name for your holiday and pick the date. Take the day off work to celebrate. Create a tradition to be observed on that day. Mark it on your calendar to be celebrated each year.

PLAYING CUPID

Write down a variety of date ideas on small slips of paper. Put each one in a different balloon. Inflate the balloons and mount them on a target.

Provide your lover with a bow and arrow and let him try to hit one of the balloons. That evening go out on the date found in the balloon which he finally pops.